1 Letters and Numbers Workbook

○ **Trace.** ✏ **Color.**

 The children trace the lines with their index finger first, and then with different colored crayons several times. Then they name the objects. Finally, the children color the pictures freely.

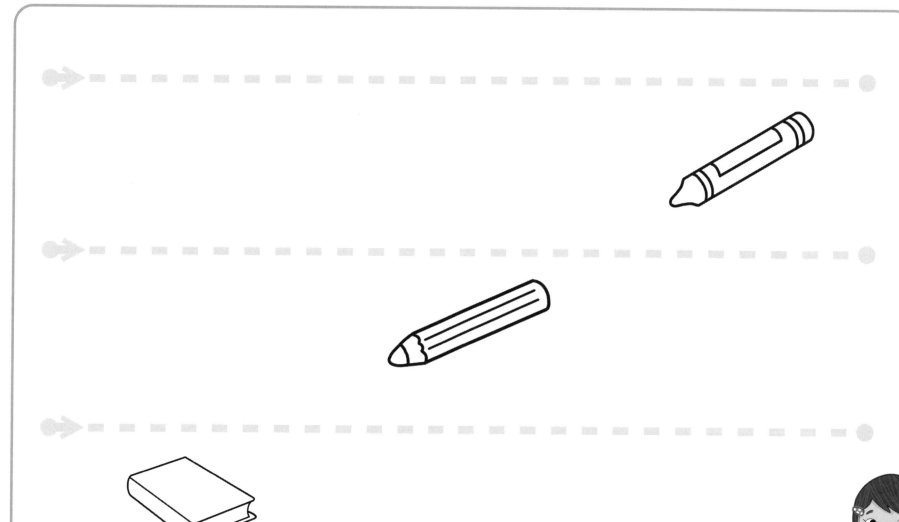

○ Trace. 💬 Say.

The children trace the lines with their index finger first, and with different colored crayons several times. Say *Kim, Dan, Kim and Dan.* The children point to the corresponding pictures and repeat.

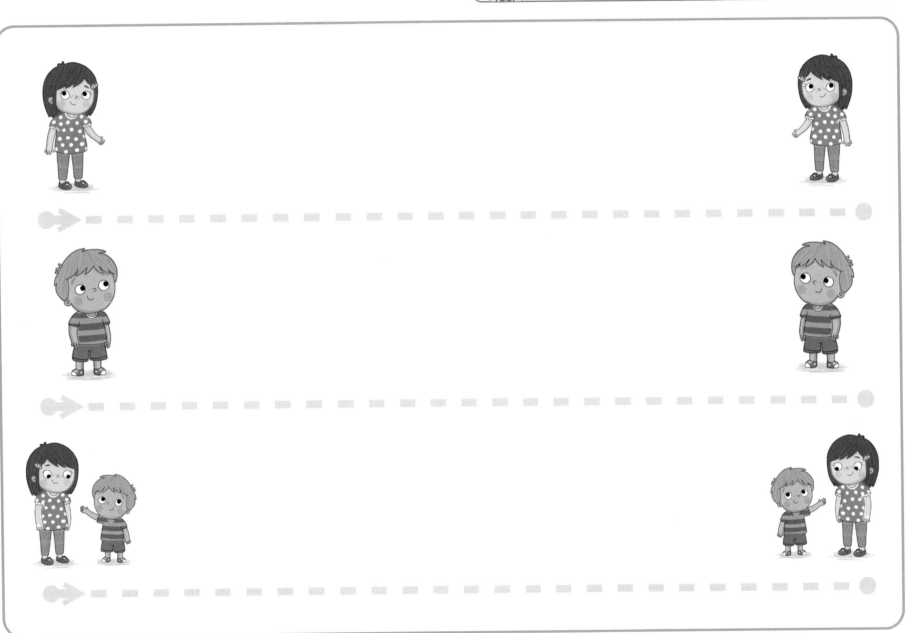

○ Trace. ✏ Color.

The children trace the lines with their index finger first, and then with different colored crayons. Then they name the pencil and the crayon, and point to the pictures. Finally, the children color the pictures freely.

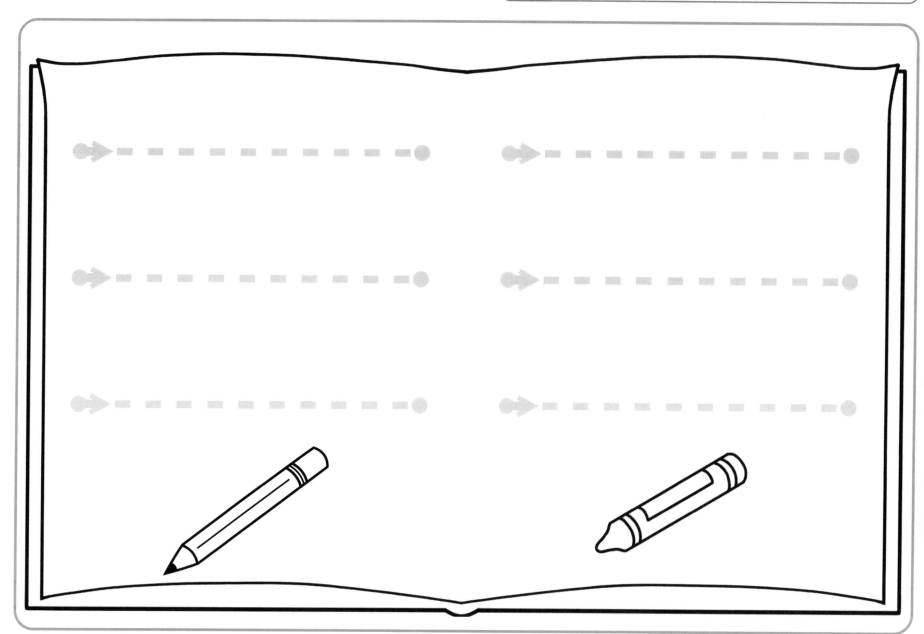

 **Count.** ⭕ **Trace.** ✏️ **Color.**

 The children name the book and count it aloud. Then they trace the number with their index finger first, and then with different colored crayons several times. Finally, the children color the book freely.

 **Count.** ⭕ **Trace.** ✏️ **Color.**

 **Count.** ◯ **Trace.**

The children point to the characters and count them aloud. Then they trace the numbers with different colored crayons several times.

◌ **Trace.** ✏ **Color.**

The children trace the lines with their index finger and with different colored crayons several times. Then they name the boys and girl and color them freely.

The children trace the lines with their index finger, and then with different colored crayons several times. Finally, the children color the pictures freely.

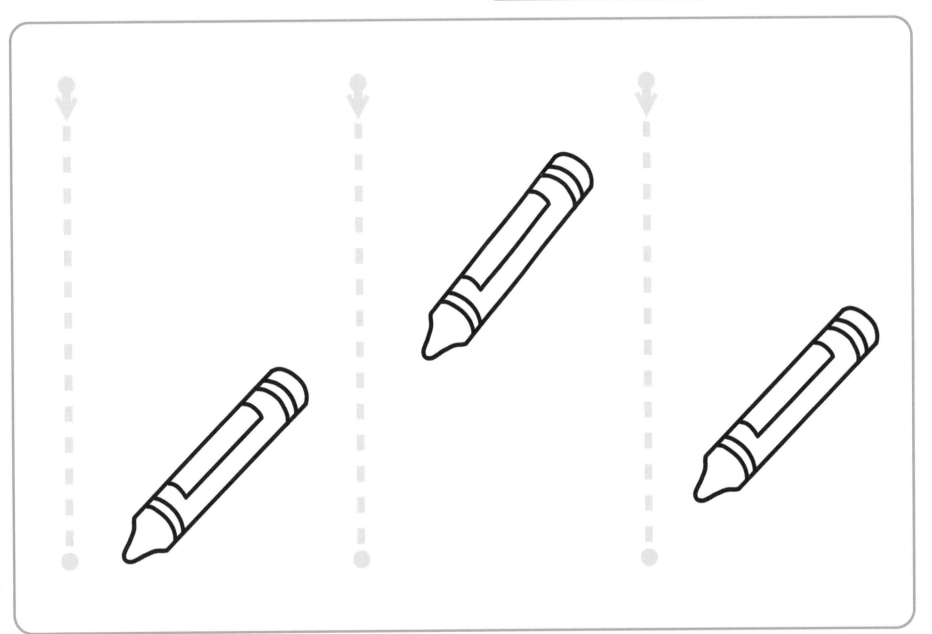

⭕ Trace. 💬 Say.

 **Count.** ⭕ **Trace.** ✏️ **Color.**

 **Count.** **Trace.** **Color.**

 The children count the girls aloud. Then they trace the number with their index finger first, and then with different colored crayons several times. Finally, the children color the picture freely.

✋ Count. ⬭ Trace. ✏️ Color.

 The children count the family members aloud. Then they trace the numbers with different colored crayons several times. Finally, they color the pictures freely.

◯ **Trace.** ✏ **Color.**

The children trace the lines with their index fingers first, and then with different colored crayons. Finally, the children name the toys and color them freely.

 # Trace. Say.

The children trace the lines with their index finger first, and then with different colored crayons. Finally, they say the patterns: *big ball, small ball, big ball, small ball; big doll, small doll …*

◯ Trace. ✏️ Color.

The children trace all the lines with different colored crayons. Then they name the toy the girls are playing with. Finally, the children color the picture.

 **Count.** ○ **Trace.** ✏ **Color.**

The children name the toys and count them aloud. Then they trace the numbers with different colored crayons several times. Finally, the children color the pictures freely.

 **Count.** **Match.** **Color.**

1 2 3 4

⭕ Trace. ✋ Count. ✏️ Color.

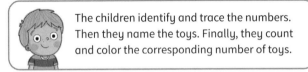

⭕ Trace. ✏️ Color.

 The children trace the circle with their index finger first, and then with different colored crayons several times. Finally, the children name the family members and the parts of the sun's face and color the picture freely.

 **Trace.** **Color.**

◯ Trace. ✏ Color.

The children trace the circles with different colored crayons several times. Then, the children name the parts of the childrens' faces and bodies and color the picture freely.

 **Count.** **Trace.** **Color.**

The children count the clowns aloud and name the parts of the face. Then they trace the number with their index finger first, and then with different colored crayons several times. Finally, the children color the pictures.

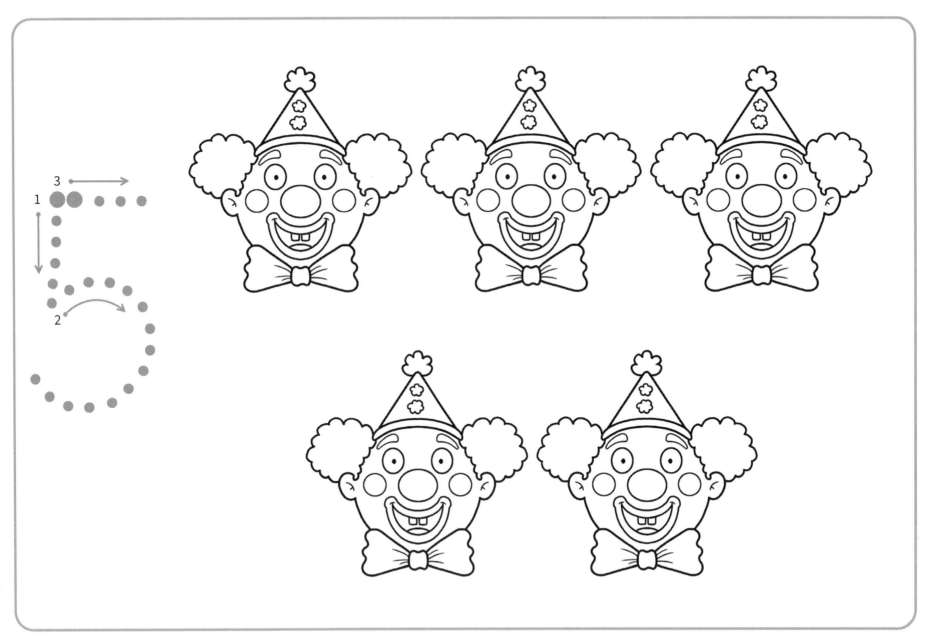

 **Count.** ◯ **Trace.** ✏ **Color.**

The children count the dolls aloud and name the parts of the body. Then they trace the number with their index finger first, and then with different colored crayons several times. Finally, the children color the picture freely.

👋 **Count.** ✏️ **Color.**

The children identify the numbers. Then they count the parts of the body aloud. Finally, the children color the pictures freely.

1 2 3 4 5 6

Unit 5

◌ **Trace.** ✏ **Color.**

The children trace the circles with their index finger first, and then with different colored crayons several times. Finally, they color the picture freely.

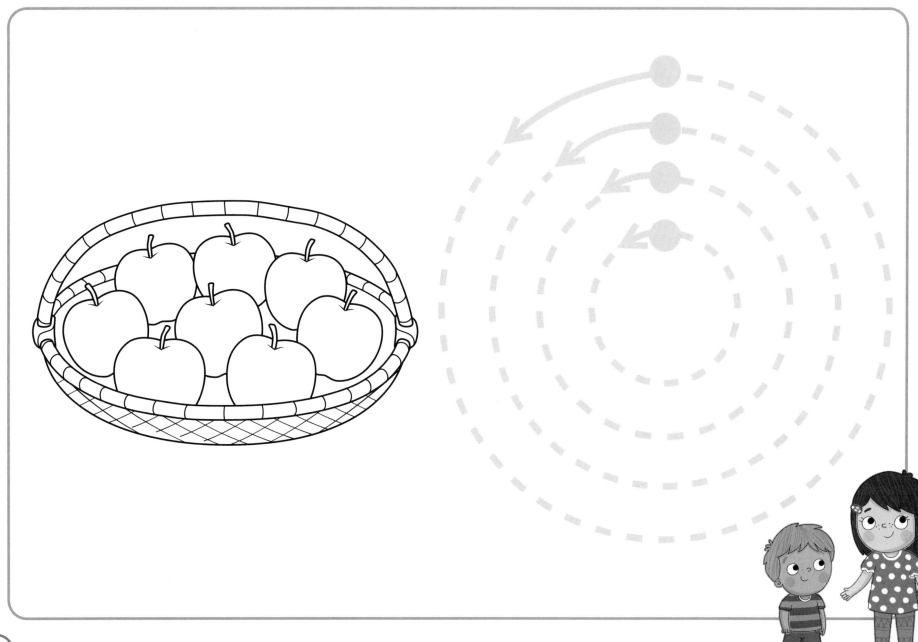

My letters

⬭ Trace. ✏ Color.

The children trace the circles with their index finger first, and then with different colored crayons several times. Finally, the children color the pictures freely.

⬭ Trace. ✏️ Color.

The children trace the circles with their index finger first, and with different colored crayons. Finally, the children color the pictures freely.

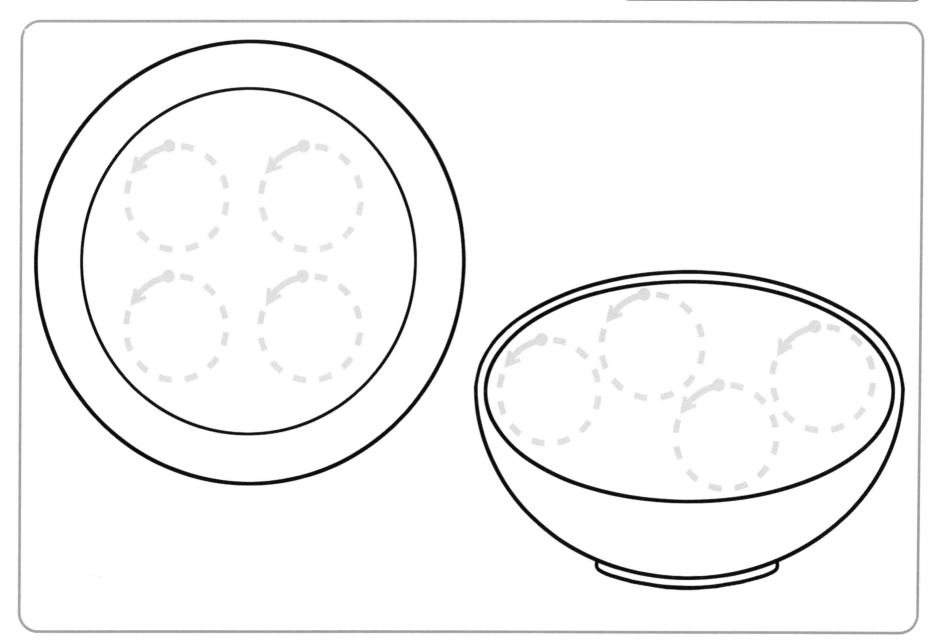

 **Trace.** **Draw.**

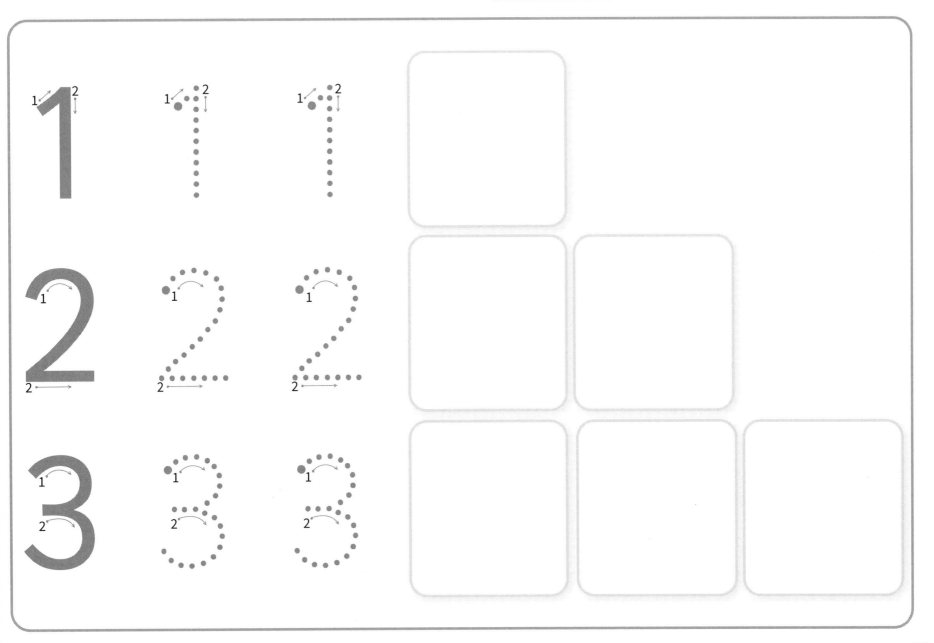

Say. ◯ Trace. ✋ Count. ✏ Color.

The children say the numbers aloud. Then they trace the numbers with different colored crayons. Finally, the children count and color the corresponding number of food items.

 **Count.** **Match.** **Color.**

1 2 3 4 5

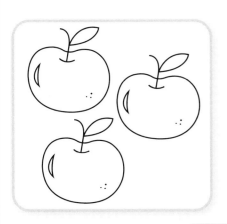

⟳ Trace. ✏ Color.

 The children trace the spiral with their index finger first, and then they trace it with different colored crayons several times. Finally, the children name the animal and color the picture freely.

 **Trace.** **Say.** ✏ **Color.**

The children trace the spirals with different colored crayons. Then they identify the animals and name them aloud. Finally, they color the picture freely.

Trace. Color.

The children trace the spirals with different colored crayons. Then they name the animals. Finally, the children color the animals freely.

My letters

Count. ◯ Trace. ✏ Color.

The children count the cats aloud. Then they trace the number with their index finger first and then with different colored crayons several times. Finally, the children color the picture freely.

 **Count.**  **Trace.** **Color.**

The children count the cats aloud. Then they trace the number with their index finger first, and then with different colored crayons several times. Finally, the children color the picture freely.

 **Count.** ◯ **Circle.** ✏ **Color.**

7   8   7   8

○ **Trace.** ✏ **Color.**

The children trace the lines with their index finger first, and then with different colored crayons several times. Finally, the children name each of the clothing items and color the pictures freely.

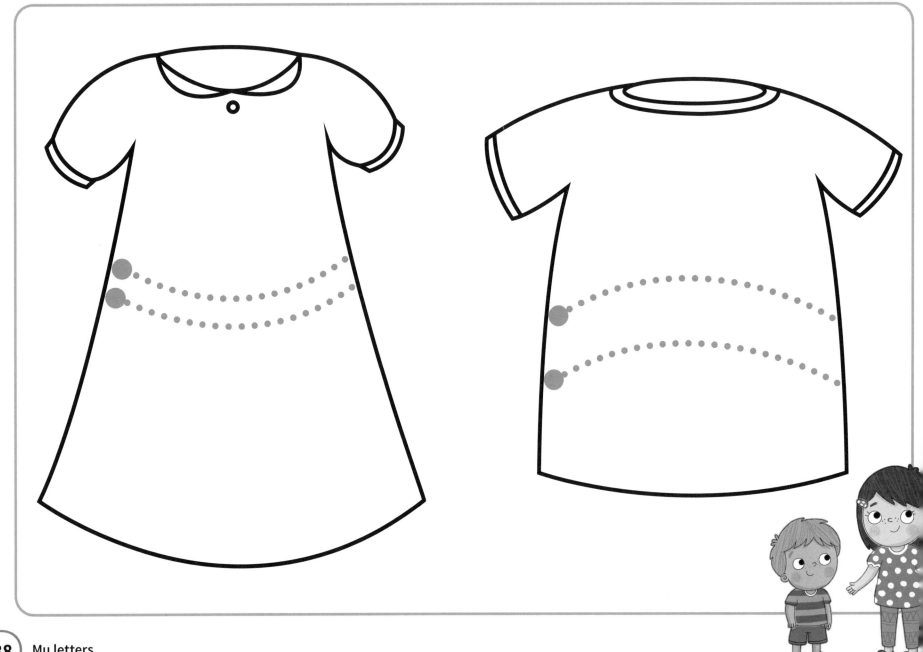

◯ Trace. ✏ Color.

The children trace the lines with different colored crayons. Next, the children name the shaded clothing items. Finally, they color the clothing items on the right.

◯ Trace. ✏️ Color.

 # Count. ⭕ Trace. ✏️ Color.

 The children count the scoops of ice cream aloud. Then they trace the numbers with different colored crayons. Finally, they color the pictures freely.

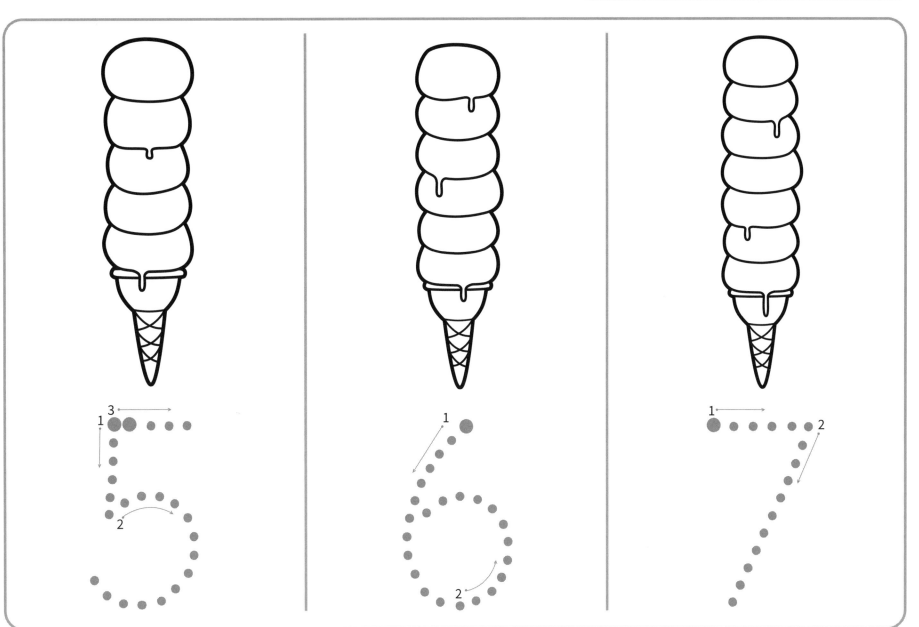

 **Count.** ◯ **Circle.** ✏ **Color.**

✋ Count. 📓 Match. ⭕ Trace.

The children count the number of shoes in each picture aloud. Then they draw lines to match the pictures with the corresponding numbers. Finally, the children trace the numbers.

 Trace. **Color.**

The children trace the "s" shape with their index finger first, and then with different colored crayons several times. Finally, the children name the vehicles and color the pictures freely.

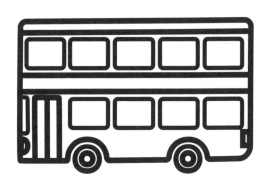

 **Trace.** **Color.**

 **Trace.** **Color.**

 # Count. Trace. Color.

The children count the cars aloud. Then they trace the number with their index finger first, and then with different colored crayons several times. Finally, the children color the pictures freely.

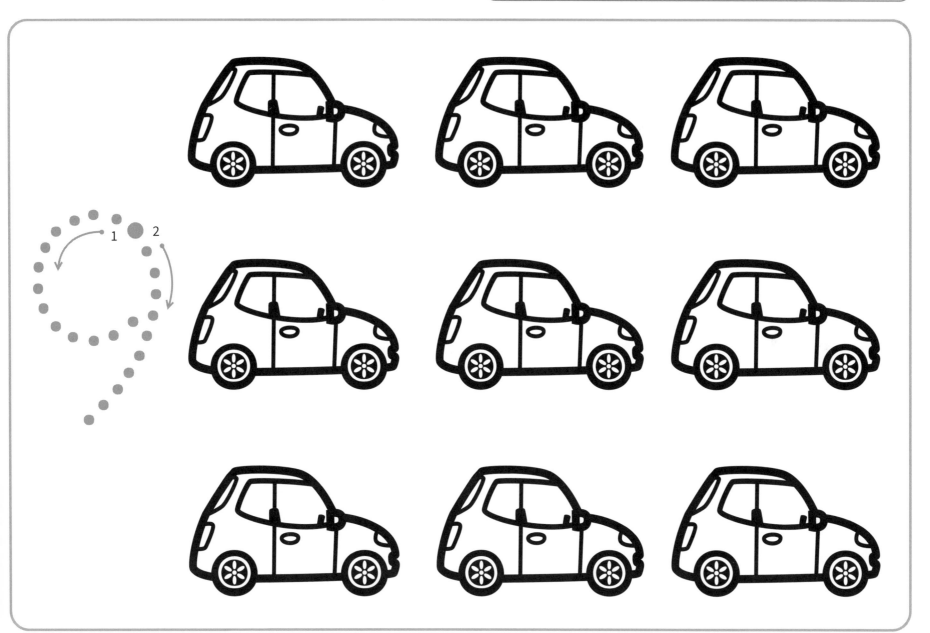

✋ Count. ⭕ Trace. ✏️ Color.

The children count the buses aloud. Then they trace the number with their index finger first, and then with different colored crayons several times. Finally, they color the pictures freely.

Count. ◯ Trace. ✎ Color.

The children count the people doing actions aloud. Then they trace the numbers with different colored crayons. Finally, they color the pictures freely.

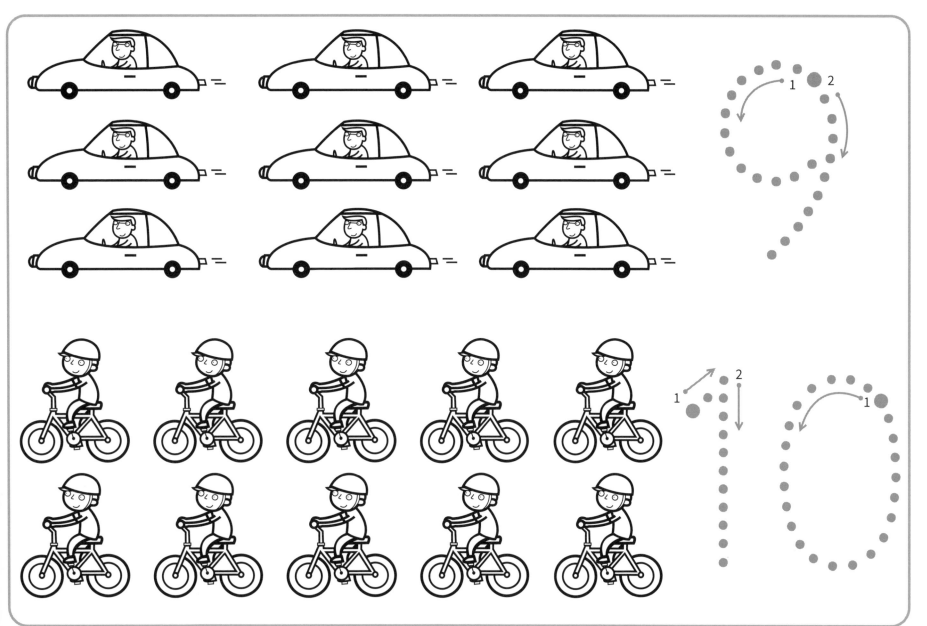

◯ **Trace.** ✏ **Color.**

 The children trace the shapes with different colored crayons. Then they name the tree and the flower. Finally, the children color the pictures freely.

⬭ Trace. ✏ Color.

The children trace the shapes with different colored crayons. Then they point to and name the animals. Finally, the children color them freely.

⬭ Trace. 🖍 Color.

👋 Count. ⭕ Trace. ✏️ Color.

The children count the pictures aloud and trace the numbers with different colored crayons. Finally, they color the pictures freely.

 Count. ◯ Trace. ✏ Color.

The children count the children in the picture. Then they trace the numbers with different colored crayons. Finally, the children color the picture freely.

✋ Count. ⭕ Trace. ✏️ Color.

 The children count each of the shapes aloud. Then they trace the numbers with different colored crayons. Finally, the children color the shapes.

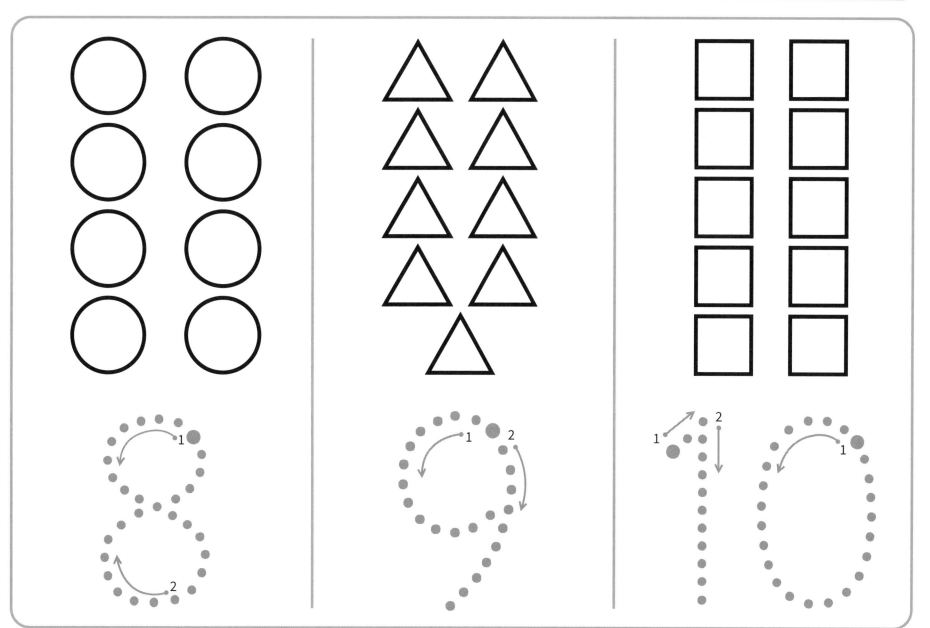

Thanks and acknowledgements

The publishers and authors would like to thank the following contributors:

Page make up by Blooberry Design and QBS Learning.
Cover concept by Blooberry Design. Cover photography by NYS444/iStock/
Getty Images.

Cover illustration by Louise Forshaw.

Illustrations by Louise Gardner, Louise Forshaw (with Collaborate artists),
Marek Jagucki, Sue King (Plum Pudding), and Bernice Lum. Icons (color, count,
draw, look, match, say, trace, tick, write) by https://thenounproject.com/icon.